Healing Through Poetry:
Beautiful Magical Scars

By Mariadaluz Fortes

Camp Street Productions
www.daluzpoetry.com

Copyright © 2024 by Mariadaluz Fortes

All rights reserved.

No part of this publication may be reproduced, distributed, or transmitted in any form or by any means, including photocopying, recording, or other electronic or mechanical methods, without the prior written permission of the publisher, except as permitted by U.S. copyright law. For permission requests, contact info@daluzpoetry.com.

Published in 2024 by Camp Street Productions
Edited by Camp Street Productions, and Madalena Taylor

Book Cover by Camp Street Productions and Adobe AI

1st edition 2024

Manufactured in the United States of America

Fortes, Mariadaluz
Healing Through Poetry: Beautiful Magical Scars

ISBN: 979-8-9878450-2-8

Dedication

In loving memory of Claudia E Moten who loved books, her Godson Mekhi and man's best friend Fluffy. Thank you for showing me the true meaning of friendship, being there for me for almost 35 years, and reminding me the importance of forgiveness and unconditional love. Most of all, thank you for loving Mekhi. Rest in paradise beautiful soul. I am extremely proud to have known you and call you a friend. May all those you left behind find peace and healing.

To all those suffering in silence. You don't have to. Please know you are loved and you can get through it. Getting help is a strength not a weakness. I pray you find courage to walk away from anything that is keeping you in pain; find a therapist who can relate to you and support you as you heal. God has a plan for you. Tap into him, so he can tap into you.

To all those who entrusted me with their pain and suffering. I hope I was able to capture your hurt and healing. Thank you for allowing me to turn tragedy into something beautiful through poetry. I hope you continue to heal and find beauty in your brokenness.

Healing Through Poetry

Table of Contents

Preface	1
Introduction	3
Identifying Broken to Finding Beauty in Healing	5
Rising in Your Trauma	17
Through the Eyes of Our Youth	25
Shades of Grief	35
Love and War	51
What's in a Name	63
Power of Words	75
Deliverance of Small Packages	81
My Sincere Thank you	91
Journal Pages	93

Healing Through Poetry

Preface

Beautiful Magical Scars encourages healing and finding beauty in the broken through poetry. It allows the reader to connect with unhealed hurt and find compassion for others. It also reminds us, our scars do not define who we are. Scars become beautiful when we see where we have been, how far we have come, forgive others, forgive ourselves, reflect, learn and move forward.

No one chooses trauma; however, we can choose to heal and live peaceful lives. What happened brought you to a dark place, but it does not have to keep you there.

Covid brought devastation, loss, and isolation. It also made it okay to seek help, make counseling and healing normal and part of everyday life. Let's continue to open doors for much needed conversations.

Healing Through Poetry

Introduction

Trauma can wrap us in depressed attire
Bury us in sorrow
And watch as we disappear
Until we are unrecognizable
We are often too broken to see it does not pour into us
No more suffering
Leaving scars and holes
As reminder of destruction
This too shall pass
Spells and storms break
Healing and forgiving restored
Holding ourselves accountable
Closing our accounts and telling trauma to hit the highway
Stakes are higher now
The same mistake we will not make
Taking responsibility
For our own happiness
Avoiding unhealthy connections for our protection
Healing is our reflection
Understand and learn from the pain
Finally letting go of the pain
Deleting and erasing learned behaviors
Psychological and physical suffering
Trading in our security blankets
And replacing them with peace and happiness
Donating kindness and forgiveness
To ignore the voices
Finding happiness within
Loving ourselves in and out of our skin

Healing Through Poetry

Identifying Broken to Finding Beauty in Healing

COVID

Forget you Covid
You took away our loved ones
Some no longer to be seen
Gone without proper goodbye
Proper burial and without closure
Others locked away with visitation restrictions
You took away our support system
And left us to deal with life and your aftermath on our own
Giving us too much time to dwell on our burdens, fears
And struggling with what was once simple
Adding frustration of technology
Family functions feeling like forced meetings
Turned into forced intervention
Because we were unable to hide our facial expressions
Further separating our relationships
With the ones we are forced to spend too much time with
Monitoring their hand washing
Falsely accusing innocent coughs of the unthinkable
Bedrooms turned into prisons
Unnecessary rules and distance at the table
Turned us into therapists
When we can't manage our own feelings
Turned us into teachers
We must remember to thank them later
Turned us into wardens sending away loved ones
Blocking needed friendships
And necessary escapes
Just when we were finally learning
To allow them room to grow and make mistakes
Earning their trust and respect

Placed back in society
Relearning basic human interactions
With invisible crayons drawing our six feet
Masked faces turned family and friends into strangers
Hiding facial expressions
Relying solely on the eyes
Unsure if it's a welcomed invitation
Or being condemned for violating rules of the new normal
Afraid to cough or sneeze
Adding new prejudice and further division to society

World is Coming to an End

Living in a world
Where we don't love God
Don't love ourselves
So how can we possibly love each other

Floods
Fires
Drowning and burning sins

Hunting little Jesus
Shooting up schools
Deleting messages
Of hopes and dreams

Making sure
Jesus
Does not win

World is coming to an end

Lacking faith
Lacking love
Lacking trust

Packing guns like goons
Shooting up churches
And movie theaters
Ending lives too soon

How do we love
An enemy
That can't be seen

Blood shedding hatred
Keeping souls and minds
In the dark and scared

Media
Social media
Aiding and abetting
Spreading and feeding
Fears

World is coming to an end

Stolen Innocence

Innocence of a child
Stolen with a smile

A secret too heavy to carry by a little heart
A life torn apart

Inflicted trauma lasting lifetime after the assault
Never understanding it was not their fault

Distrust
Mistrust
No trust

Confusion turns to hate
Affecting their mental state

Drugs and alcohol to drown the pain
Wasting their brain and going insane

Anything not to feel the pain
Innocent and fragile heart forever stained

Silent Cries

You may be deep inside
But she still finds a way to hide
Dancing away the pain
Sexing away the pain
Moving and running from the pain
Some want all of her
None get all of her
Smiling to hide the pain
Lying to the pain
Hoping to cut ties with the pain
Your pleasures met
Using sex as a way to forget
Bathing to drain away the pain
Washing away the pain
Scrubbing away the pain
Satisfied your needs then you fell asleep
Never heard her weep
No way out of the pain
Nowhere to hide the pain
No escape from the pain
Loss of innocence left a stain that will remain
Needing to be fed until she stops or ends up dead
Forced to feel the pain
Sit with the pain
Deal with the pain
Understand and learn from the pain
Finally letting go of the pain

Seeds of Insecurity

Black and white women
Have been unfairly divided
Since slavery
Black women raped by white men
Giving birth to a new breed of people
Not knowing where they fit in
White women stood helpless
Planting seeds of insecurity
Black men stood helpless
Now planting their seeds
Of insecurity and self hatred
In the wombs of white women
White men learning to love the faces
Of their ancestor's sins
While black women
Plant seeds of their own insecurity
Different times
Same outcome
Another generation
Who don't know where they fit in
Only difference
Is the color of the mother's skin
Black and white women
It's time we unite
In sisterhood and motherhood
Our down fall and only enemy
Is our commitment to our men
Instead of ourselves
And each other

Coffin of Hopes and Dreams

Living in a fishbowl
Hearts and souls on display
Insecure thoughts
Swimming with fear
Inhaling rejection
Exhaling hopes and dreams
To a toxic environment
No encouragement
No nourishment
To grow and reach
Its full potential
Floating and dissipating
Into nothing
Ensuring
You stay in a box
Society built for you

Pouring Damage

Empty beer cans
Stumbling over
Spilling sorrow

Dressed up wine bottles
Steady pouring
Nowhere to go and no one to follow

Wasted and reckless
Feeling low
No self esteem to borrow

Hoping there is no tomorrow

Drowning in tears
Caused by fears and regrets
Pouring into an early grave too shallow

Too weak to climb up the ladder of hope
So you hide it with scope
As you carry your cargo

Too broken to see it's not pouring into you
It's you pouring damage into you
Look at your shadow

Little Black Boys

Everyday he is reminded
He cannot play with his water guns
He does not understand
It is not just a toy

It is an excuse
For cops
To shoot
Little black boys

His skin color makes him a target
Preconceived notions
Wants him in a jail cell, a grave
Or drugged up so they can control him

His favorite hoodie
Makes him a threat
He can never collect
On society's debt

A King died
So he can live a dream
But finds himself
Living a nightmare

Healing Through Poetry

Rising in Your Trauma

Pain is Not a Fair Game

My heart time traveled to defame
Expose your abuser's domain
And username

Inflame their power burning to ashes with no insurance claim
No longer to lay claim

Your heart will remain
And it knows why I came

To proclaim and end the shame
Your innocence to reclaim

How can so much pain live in a little frame
I am sorry they caused you pain
You are not the blame

Let's rename what you became
Hurt is not your first name
Damage is not your surname

If they hit you with that nickname
Or call you out your name
Hit them with a counterclaim

Exclaim and declaim their war game
Victory will never be their end game

Beautiful Magical Scars

Play them like a board game
Protect your peace like a Queen in a chess game

Maintain a survival mindframe
Your spirit they cannot break or tame

Rise up to fame
You overcame
You are NOT your pain

Bridge

I first saw you on a bridge

I was trying to bridge the gap between pain and healing
While you pretended to jump off one
To bridge the gap between broke and riches

I first saw you on a bridge

I struggle to cross my bridge
As you pull tricks in a game of bridge

I first saw you on a bridge

Standing in a path of disappointments
Hoping to overcome
And make a difference
But all you wanted was to divide

I first saw you on a bridge

I long to see pain cross the bridge to healing
You remain to build a land of suffering that prolongs healing

I first saw you on a bridge

Water under my bridge
As you burn your bridge
When your bridge loan is due
I hope you find healing too

I first saw you on a bridge

Boundaries

Feeling like I have no say
No control
Hurts so bad
All I can do is pray
Can't climb out of this hole
My wishes they won't obey
Sucking out my soul

Needing to do some self-care
Protect my mental space
Make them aware
They can no longer bring me to that place
Setting rules of engagement deemed fair
Strengthening relationships with grace

Avoid unhealthy connection
No longer to be degraded
For my protection
Disrespect not tolerated
Healing is my reflection

Allowing others to know my limits
And appropriate behaviors
Drawing a firm line to eliminate
Unkind treatment or favors

Making it clear
Where I end and where you begin
Being used has been unfair
Manipulated by those who claimed to be a friend
Violates my boundaries and you will not win

From Broken to Valuable

Broken hearts
Pieced back together
With gold
Extracted
From kind words
And selfless acts
Melted and turned into joy
That was once tears
Now washing away pain and hurt
And replacing it with
Peace and happiness
Rejoice and heal
For the heart
Is more valuable
Once broken
Now pieced together
By joy
Pure as gold

**Poem based on ancient Japanese art form called Kintsugi used to repair broken pottery with gold making the piece more valuable

Lost Sons

The first sound a lost son hears
Are the cries of his mother giving birth to him

The last sound a lost son hears
Is the sound of his mother pleading with God to spare her son's life
And begging him not to leave her

Too many of our sons have been lost
To mental health, drugs, the streets, court systems, prison, violence

Countless sons left without a father
Sent out in the world without guidance
Facing struggles of life in silence
And without support

Labeled and stereotyped
Treated badly
With nothing to lose
And everything to prove

The answers to many prayers
Restoration of hopes and dreams
Are held within the first lost son called Jesus

Let's put him back in our hearts
Let's put him back in our homes
Let's put him back in our schools

So we can find and heal our lost sons

Through the Eyes of Our Youth

The Kid With Two Backpacks

I carry two backpacks
One has my school supplies
But the heavy one is a target on my back
It is full of things that keeps me from being my best
Worries of home and food insecurities
Fear always telling me
I can't do it
I am not good enough
Parents and teachers expectations that are too high
Or not having the tools to meet them
You can see how it affects me
It causes some of you to pick on me
Walking down the hall having all eyes on me
With false ideas of who I am
I want to scream
But nothing comes out
Sometimes all I need is a smile and a kind word
It helps me get through the day
And oftentimes I forget my heavy bag
Of self doubt, worries, and fears
And I am able to enjoy the remaining of the day

It's Going to be Okay

It's been a bad day
Nothing going my way
Looking for a getaway
Or hideaway
Feeling like a castaway
Troubles fades away
So they say
When things don't go my way
Get two friends on a three way
At the problem we will chip away
Attacking until it breaks away
Or we make a way
Telling these problems, I'm not a milky way
At me it will not eat away
Taking good days off layaway
Closing my account and telling my troubles to hit the highway
Skies don't stay gray
Is not another cliche
Celebrating like it's my birthday
And looking forward to better days

Replacing Treasures for Freedom

They robbed me of my security blanket

Don't they know I deposited fears
In my security blanket

Don't they know I wrapped my insecurities
In my security blanket

Don't they know I wiped tears
In my security blanket

They robbed me of my security blanket

Don't they know I hid blame
In my security blanket

Don't they know I entrusted mistrust
In my security blanket

Don't they know I stained guilt
In my security blanket

Don't they know I buried shame
In my security blanket

They robbed me of my security blanket

They robbed me …… wait
They saved me from my security blanket

Job Corps

A two year program
Where a teen can get a GED and a trade
Earning while learning
A second chance
At normalcy
Building friendships
Dorm life drama
Doing chores
Learning leadership
Gaining your own room
Cafeteria catwalk
Recreation room excitement
Pool table corner shots
Reneging in spades
Dances with DJs scratching the hottest beats
Field trips sign up sheets
Bowling and knocking down challenges
Roller skating your way to new love
Van runs
Serving as needed breaks
Fun in the city
Developing a sense of self
Realizing there is more to life
Selected few enrolled in college
Ending your term
Starting anew
With a firm sense of adulthood
And accomplishments

Healing Through Poetry

Wrestling With Fear

Fear has ahold of me
It told me
I am unable to forgive

I failed to realize
What God gave

It knows and sees
The greatness in me
God's vision for me

God says
I am capable
I have what it takes

Fear why do you still have ahold of me

What is the bondage
I must release myself from

Yes God
It's you
I want to please

I can't stay still
They say
I will feel the holy spirit
Like a breeze

Beautiful Magical Scars

It must of missed me
And now
Blowing in the trees
Fear
Why are you still here

What is the message
You don't want me to hear

My fear is not failing
My fear is succeeding

Holding myself accountable
For what I allowed you to take

Stakes are higher now
The same mistake
I will not make

Fear
I no longer want or need you here

Love Letters to Our Youth

You are plenty
And more than enough
Don't allow anyone to make you believe otherwise

Always remember that bullies are unhappy with themselves
It's never about you, so lend them a smile
Lead by example and show them kindness

Surround yourself with positivity
And those who share your same interest
You have everything it takes to succeed
Everyone measures success differently
So only compete with yourself

Strive to be better than you were yesterday
You will not always get it right and that's okay

Keep in mind your parents may not have all the answers
But they love you and want what is best for you
Give each other space and grace
Be respectful and offer a helping hand

Do what you love and what makes you happy
Remove I can't from your vocabulary
Replace perfect with practice

Focus on today and leave yesterday in the past
Don't allow fears to steal your tomorrow
Being afraid may last moments
While regrets may last a lifetime

Making mistakes is a part of learning and a part of life
Reflect
Learn
And move on

Knowing you can and will do better
Keep learning
Keep growing
Keep doing you
Keep loving you

Shades of Grief

Mourning the Living

I mourn a carefree childhood
This generation will never know
What smelling like the outside
And coming home before street lights come on

I mourn family events
That included every generation and relation
Cousins now strangers
When they became twice removed

I mourn the job
That overlooked me
They will never see my full potential
Or experience my passion

I mourn the lover
Who dwells above ground
X marks the spot
But the only treasure found was failed love

I mourn unmanaged relationships
Resolution was one call away
I did not have the courage or too prideful to make
Now all that is left are unspoken words

I mourn a society
With a false sense of security
Crowds and flights
Now comes with an exit plan and counseling

Beautiful Magical Scars

I mourn the living
Who die before they truly live
Putting paychecks before family
And investing in everything but themselves

I mourn lost souls
Who do not know the power of prayer
Or choose life after death
With the Prince of Peace

I mourn the living

Universal Language of Grief

Death comes like a thief
Collecting dreams of the deceased
Trying to take found memories in its valise

Leaving us in disbelief
Speaking universal language of grief
Collecting cards of rest in peace

Photo collage masterpiece
Casket turned into centerpiece
Say your peace and take a seat

Buckets of tears with no relief
Dripping on our picture tees and neckpiece
Cars line the streets to Heaven's Gate lead by police

Repass, this too shall pass as you release
Let their life's work be the conversation piece
In time the pain will decrease

Cancer

Carelessly and slowly destroying people we love
Anger consumes broken hearts and lives
Never easing up on pain and suffering
Countless plans delayed or canceled
Eternal rest you placed upon so many
Returning and wanting to claim more

So forget you cancer
Go back to the hell you came from
We refuse to give more
You no longer have consent or permission
To take what is not yours
Surrender and restore our peace

No more lives to be stolen
No more broken hearts
No more suffering
No more removed limbs
Leaving scars and holes
As reminder of your destruction

My Angel

You are my Angel
I have looked up to you all my life
Now you are looking to me to carry on your memories
To carry on your smile and your love

My Angel

I see you in my dreams
I feel you in my heart
I still smell your sweet perfume
But it leads nowhere

My Angel

My eyes are open
But I cannot see
Help me understand
Why you are not here with me

My Angel

Tears of Domestic Violence

Her smile
Still illuminates
Circumstances of her death
Still cast sadness
Memories of her
Sometimes foggy
Inflamed anger
Desperately trying to forget
Details of her death
The burning building
Concealing his crimes
Still stand
Hearts collapse in its darkness
Paralyzed
Before falling to tears
Fifteen years later
Still feeling helpless
Visions of her swollen body
Twenty-seven stab wounds
Continues
To disturb our peace
And faith in mankind and justice system
Showering in tears of domestic violence
Soaking
In painful and heavy reality
Shattering countless lives
Her killer emerges after sabbatical from life behind bars
But it is her loved ones
Who are sentenced to life
Without her

Our Precious Gem We Call Tia Bia

One of three sisters taking turns caring for Grandma
And keeping the family together
Three becomes two as she leaves a hole that can't be filled
She loved a generation of nieces and nephews
Who sat around her living room floor on Christmas Eve
Gift wrapping covered the floor
Like a rug made from happiness of children
Multiple generations under her roof as one
One family
One love
One gift of togetherness
Making memories lasting a lifetime
Some of our fondest memories
Her rolling a cart of goodies as a RI Hospital worker
Helping patients feel at ease
Her sliding down South Court on her bottom in the snow
Was how she made it down the hill
Sunday dinners feeling like Thanksgiving
Turkey with the works tasting like joy
A wing saved especially for her
She came to United States but never forgot
Where she came from or her people
She sent money to churches and children on a regular
If Tia Bia was here she would say
Don't cry for her as she lived a full life
She married the love of her life
Who came with a ready made family
The child she longed for gave her grandchildren
And became her caregiver
She traveled the country and the world
With her beloved and friends

Wings that Delivered Compassion

We were two women he fell in love with
Combined we were the perfect woman
Produced beautiful children

We had the same beautiful heart
The same captivating smile
The same reason to give up and the same reason to keep going

Had we met outside of him we would of been great friends
Bickering kept us at a distance
Lies and whispers kept his secret safe

Spells break
Storms break
Communication breakdown restored

A special person by the name of Michele
Reminded us the meaning of compassion
Earning her wings before going to her resting place

Danny

Looking out the window
To get a glimpse of your friendly face
Only to find an empty space

The chair your body dwelled in for hours
While listening to music
And enjoying the company of loved ones
Now empty

Our hearts overspill with sympathy
Lifting our cups toasting
To Danny

Enjoying our brandy
Patriots and Red Sox scoring for Danny making twenty
As for Memories we have plenty

Assigned Pain and Memories

I can no longer
Call your number
It's been reassigned
But the pain
Of your departure
Still remain
Deleting your number
Does not delete
The pain
And will never
Delete memories
They are all that remain
Forever assigned
And forever
Mine

Expired Time

Gathering around a bedside
Expressing concealed feelings
Speaking life into the "what if" of regrets
Consoling stubborn pride
Trying to buy back time
Wishing for a do over
Being still in the moment
Realizing time has passed
And can't be revived

Last Sound of Regrets

Being in your last moments
Fighting for your life
Trying to let go
Wanting to let go
Needing to let go
Holding on to loved ones words
As they hold on to your hand
Looking for peace and comfort
To transition over
Taking your last breath
Only to hear your loved ones
Expressing the "I am sorry"
That should have been offered long ago

Focus on My Smiling Face

You came to me in the still of the night
Your face I see but I cannot feel your touch
Stop crying you say
I am in a better place
Close your eyes and focus on my smiling face
I want to trust what you say
But last time……. You went away
Close your eyes you repeated
So I did
A lifetime of memories took over my body
I felt warm
All of a sudden you were real
I felt your touch
Your smile
Warm as the sun
I was in a peaceful place and I did not want to leave
But you insisted I listened to what you had to say
Whenever you need me
Close your eyes and focus on my smiling face
You started to move away
The more I reached out
The further you went away
All I could hear was
Close your eyes and focus on my smiling face
I wanted to obey
But I was so afraid
Don't go
Please don't go I begged
But all I could hear was
Close your eyes and focus on my smiling face

Beautiful Magical Scars

When I stopped crying
My eyes closed
There you were
Just like you said you would be

Love and War

From HIStory to Our Story

I look in the mirror and see her eyes
She looks in the mirror and sees my smile
We have too much in common
Some of our flaws the same
Some of our attributes the same
Could it be why he fell in love with the both of us
Choosing to end the drama and the history
Leaving it all in the past
Taking his out of history
And making it our story
We are more than two women
That share children
And once loved the same man
Choosing more for ourselves and our children
Closing a chapter
Of the unsaid and moving on
With the smiles, bright eyes of our children
All of the good he saw in us, we see in them
Had we showed each other compassion back then
Who knows what would have happened or taken place
We were destined to be in each other's lives
Somehow intertwined never understanding why

Cause & Effect of Your Smile

Her words painted a picture of your smile
Hairs stood up on the back of my neck
Shivers ran down my spine

Memories overwhelmed my body
I knew it was your smile
It was tattooed in my mind

The twenty year old girl in me
You met so long ago
Cried tears of regret

The forty year old woman in me
You found again
Cried tears of betrayal

The fifty year old sentimental me
Wonders
Did you see me in her

Lost Key

I changed the locks into my life
But forgot your key has entry to my heart

Sweet irony of love lost
Flowing like poetry

What good is a changed life
Without a changed mindset and heart

Tears of misery
Needing and wanting company

How do we live a life
Without mending a broken heart

Facing a choice and help the enemy
Is it love or human decency

Buried in Sorrow

Love tried to kill me
Slowly and painfully
Crushing my spirit
Breaking my heart

Taking every ounce of my joy
And every breath in my lungs
Drowning me in my own tears
Until I was broken and empty

It wrapped me in depressed attire
Buried me in sorrow
And watched as I disappeared
Until I was unrecognizable

Love could not kill me
Love is pure and comes from a powerful source
Love does not destroy
Love can only restore

Prince of My Heart

Prince of my heart
Sorry I kept you waiting
We have been apart
Far too long and caring
For the wrong counterpart
Endured all the hurting
Hoping for a fresh start
Love's failed history ending
Giving our hearts a jump-start

Dear Future Husband

You have been let down
Put down
And broken down

Held hostage
By the wrong spouse
Poor decisions or bad habits

I need you to look in the mirror
And see God's plan for you
You are not your bad choices or habits

I pray for you
I ask God to give you courage
To walk away from everything holding you back

You are worthy and deserving of happiness
Life was not meant to be spent alone or unhappy
I will wait patiently until our hearts unite

Marriage

Before I call you husband
You need to know
Our names were written in the sand
With purpose to show

We will become one
Rain or shine
It will not always be fun
I am yours and you are mine

You will be more than a spouse
We need a home
Not just a house
From our love we cannot stray or roam

Our union
Is more than rights and obligations
Not even In-Laws can ruin
It must remain intact despite all situations

It will take teamwork
With love and respect
We can make this dream work
Our bond we must protect

Ring of Trust

                My King

A Queen's promises to him
Is as strong as the ring
Of trust
If that ring
Is weak or broken
So are her promises

                My King

                                  What glue
                              Bonds your ring
                                    Of trust
                              Will your words
                              Prove to be true
                    Or will they turn into dust

                My King

Don't let that ring rust
Keeping promises
Are a must

                My King

                                  What is a pie
                                    Without
                                      A crust

                My King

Broken promises
Are just
As broken as the King

                My King

                                  What glue
                              Bonds your ring
                                  Of trust

Provoked Lust

Awoke minds and hearts
Heavy with regret
Spoke no hurt
Betrayal we soon forget

Provoked lust
Breaking out into sweat
Soak the honey pot
Collect love's debt

Distracted by rough
"You are mine" grip
Invited softness of his tongue
On my inner thigh and V lip

Injected the tip
Rejoined at the hip

Feelings once dead
Lies no longer wed
Reunions naysayers dread

Hearts healed
As we make and lay in our bed

Passionate kisses
Secrete wishes
Complete and secure Mr. and Mrs.

Love

Spending quality time
Expressing affection
Knowing how and where
To touch me
Displaying actions and behaviors
Letting me know
You are committed to me
I can trust
You will protect me
Allowing me to feel safe
Be vulnerable
Giving me room to grow
Forgiving me
When I make mistakes
Listening and communicating
Tackling conflict
Through our love language

What's in a Name

Mama

Mothers
Always
Make
A way

Her feet tired from walking
To and from work
Her legs support her as they know
Her family depends on her
Her bottom stiff from sitting
In front of a machine for ten hours
Her back pain pours like rain
But her shoulders carry her through
Her heart skips a beat
When she realizes her older children
Took care of the little ones
Her arms longing to hold her babies
Her sore hands transfer love with every touch
As her lips softly kisses sleeping faces
Her eyes see a bright and better future
Her mind reminds her why she does it
And prepares her to do it all again tomorrow

Papa

Parenting a generation in a new world
Adjusting to a different culture
Preparing grandchildren to preserve our language
Admired by so many

A police officer by trade
Hand weaving baskets and playing the drums
Was his passion
Helping young men migrate to all parts of the world
Was his gift
He played so many roles
But being Papa was his pride and joy
Fifteen years older than his wife allowed him
To spend quality time with their children after retirement
Teaching them more than arithmetics
Leading by example and demonstrating
Doing what is right even when no one is looking
Being honest and trustworthy
Keeping your word and being a true friend
Work ethics and the benefits of hard work
Holding on to people instead of things
Living with principle and practice
After you are gone
People will not remember what you did
But how you made them feel

Ruth

Radiant
Unforgettable
Trustworthy
Helping hands

Hanging plants high
Beautiful curtains below
Decorative pillows placed just right
Vibrant green couch displaying your caring heart
Countless books stand tall and proud
Supporting children as they read out loud
Your love has no end
United hearts we stand
Memories flowing faster than tears
As we fear
Not having you near
Your love can do no wrong
Not ready for your love to be taken away
Please stay
Please stay
As we sing along
Where you wanting to go
We cannot come along
Extending our song
Your trip prolong
Stay strong
Stay strong
As you end our song
Saying with Nana is where you belong

Claudia

Caring
Loving
Always
Unapologetically
Demanding
Idealistic
Actions

> To know her is to love her
> There is no way to love her without knowing her
> Thirty plus year friendship
> And not a dull moment
> The Thelma
> To my inner Louise
> Fighting my battles when I did not have the strength
> Or pull me away with three words "lets go scrappy"
> Always there when I needed her
> Countless secrets and endless memories
> From building TV stands
> To hiding each other's debit cards
> Because "Freddy was always already"
> Thirty days hospital stay
> The only thing she frowned upon was cheating in cards
> Her loyalty was never a question
> But it wasn't until we both received a blessing
> Of a little boy by the name of Mekhi
> That sealed our friendship for life

Alipio

Another
Love
Intense
Poem leaving me
Intoxicated
On Cloud 9

                                        He has a way with words
                            Claiming action like those verbs
                       Describing my needs like adverbs

                                              He's like a herb
             Seasoning the sentence you haven't heard
            Got me hanging on to his every word

                                    His poems he serves
                                          So Superb
                                   Do not disturb
                                      As I absorb

                            Obsession with his words
Calling out his name made my man kick me to the curb
                                      It's all a blurb
                                   Am not perturb
                        His words are a healing herb

Rosy

Radiant
Opened hearted
Supportive
Yours

                                             She rises before the sun
                                             She grinds but still shines

                                                      Bettering her life
                               Touching so many lives in the process

                      Children blessed by her kindness and gifts
                                  Babies calmed by her touch

                                             She rises before the sun
                                           She does not need the sun

                                                        She is the sun

Thomas

Totally
His
Own
Man
Always
Sincere

An engagement ring
Did not keep him away
Being told I was getting married
Did not keep him from insisting I was the one for him
Flowers, lunch, persistency
And the most beautiful smile
I have ever seen, won my heart
Learning true love is not only expressed in words
It's shown when a man lets you drive his prized Cadillac
Knowing you might put some scratches and dents on it
But the only scratches and dents he is not okay with
Are the ones on the heart of the woman he loves
Not wise or brave enough
I let go of the best thing
That ever happened to me
Fear is a battle
We must fight
In order to win the war in love and in life

Bardowell

Bobby Brown Fan
A Friend until the end
Roller skating
Dancing
On every floor
World he travels
Enjoying
Loved ones
Leaving no plate untouched

> Became friends in Job Corps
> Struggling through drivers ed
> Each failing twice
> Never letting her know
> She was his crush
> But his actions did show
> A friendship he did not rush
> Dancing to "Tender Rony"
> Always real
> Still friends without a kiss to steal
> Because he was never phony

Stacy

Safely
Talking
About
Concerns
You need to heal from

> God provided me an angel
> By the name of Stacy
> Giving me tools to sort how I feel
> And remove any label
> Given by society
> Making sure my happiness they can no longer steal

Sisters

Siblings
Inspiring
Special
Tenderhearted
Essential
Relatable
Supportive

Sisters by flesh and blood
Connected by unending love
Friends by genuine choice
Pure and natural as our inner and outer beauty
The good, crazy, bad and ugly
Covered by unconditional love
Honesty without fear, discomfort, or judgment
Time holds no bound
We may not speak or see each other daily
But when we are together
Our passionate kindred spirited energy becomes stronger
Making our bond powerful and unbreakable
Not even death can break
We lost our sweet and precious Julie
But she lives on in our smiles and hearts
She is sometimes seen in one sister's eyes
Heard in another sister's advice and laughter
And her kindness is felt in our actions
Making our relationship imperfectly perfect and timeless

Power of Words

Intimacy

Intimate
Natural
a**T**mosphere
In which
fa**M**iliarity
Affection
Closeness
Allows **Y**ou to see into my soul

Music

Memories, feelings, and pain
Unleashed
Speaking healing
If used
Correctly

Wish

Without planning
Incorporating "learn and move on" mentality
Setting goals
Honing in on ambition and desire to succeed

A wish is just fairy dust and a tale too tall to reach

Fear

Facing what scares you
Entering into a new chapter of your life
Allowing yourself to navigate life without
Regrets

Fault

Facing
Actions
Unsatisfactory
Leaving room for growth
Taking responsibility

Alone

A homeless heart
Longing for comfort
Of belonging
Nurturing and healing emotional wounds
Ending the cycle in order to find happiness

Hate

Hostility
Anger
Threatening behavior
Extreme dislike

Misplaced feelings
Of bigotry
Due to fear
Insecurity
Mistrust
Or lack of understanding something different

War

Without respect, communication and common decency
All those in power will
Renege on promises of peace

Depression

Depriving yourself of
Everything because of not being able to
Properly handle and deal with
Reality and temporary situations
Experiencing loss or lack of doing what you love
Suppressing your feelings
Symptoms of mood swings
Increased time spent alone or sleeping making you an
Outcast in your own life unless you realize that feeling sad is
Normal side effect of life

Healing

Helping yourself by finding
External
Assistance
Learning to forgive and move on
Implementing boundaries and expectations
Navigating through life and relationships
Growing and knowing you can only control your own reactions

Deliverance of Small Packages

Bare Skin

The you that would not allow you to win
The story you could no longer spin
Unhappiness got comfortable and set in
Making loving you a sin
Find happiness within
Love you in and out of your own skin

Crocodile Tears

Crocodile tears
No longer scares
Because nobody cares
Looking for new volunteers
Still wet behind the ears
Playing musical chairs
Unauthorized shares
Unloading fears
On its peers
Until music it no longer hears

My Crazy Glue

I live in a tool box
With a bunch of nuts
Rusty bolts
And screws so loose
My crazy glue
Won't be able to hold them together

Calm Seas Broken Ships

Our relationship stopped moving
And became a situationship

You neglected your duties to our partnership
And became a receivership

We should of held on to our friendship
But lost sight of it and choose companionship

Forgot we all have hardship
And hold membership to a sinking ship

Marriage of the Mind and Heart

My heart ordained
A life with you
But my mind
Could not submit
To an arrangement
Where I am not
Seen or heard

Exposed Emptiness

Our brokenness
Intertwined
Never making us whole
Exposing the emptiness
Comforting a damaged soul
Allowing you to see
What love looks like
Allowing me to finally see
What it can never be

Exposed Harm to Unprepared Minds

Children acting like adults
Due to
Being exposed
To things
They aren't ready for
Turned
Into adults
Acting like children
Due to
Things they weren't
Prepared for

Dear Absent Parents

Your child needs both parents
You each come with gifts and lessons
Put together to make your child succeed
In a world where love is lacking
Your child needs double the dose
Do your part and stop slacking

Meanwhile

That person who greets all with a smile
Will walk a mile
To help you reconcile
That is their style

Their presence worthwhile
Happy profile
Always gentile
Never hostile

Even when problems pile
Or troubles line in a file
You will never see their pain or trail
Worrying others is not their lifestyle

Even the strong get weak once in awhile
Who do they turn to when they are fragile
So many contacts in their mobile
But no one to dial

My Pawtucket Poetry

My Pawtucket Poetry is safe
It provides a place with listening ears
And no judgment

My Pawtucket Poetry is healing
It continues to help me face my hurt
And find ways to move past it

My Pawtucket Poetry is wisdom
It lends me words
When I cannot find any

My Pawtucket Poetry is home
It gives me courage
And people who share my passion

Healing Puzzle

Healing is like a puzzle
But unlike other puzzles
It cannot start from the outside
The work must begin on the inside
Working on yourself
Carefully choosing people
Deserving of being around you
Filling the missing pieces
With self worth
Self love
Trust and respect
Setting clear expectations
And boundaries
Instead of walls

Spring

Days become longer
And marches old man winter
Out of equinox

Taking away darkness
And restoring
Equal amount of light

Allowing the sun
To melt away
Gloom of cold weather

Returning death of past seasons
Beneath ground

The earth welcomes
Absorbs and embraces
The lifeless

Her tears turn to rain
And transforms old into new

Blooming
And giving back
Joy, hope, life, and beauty

Rebirth

Broken minds
Wounded spirits
Collecting shattered hearts
Has the soul
Exfoliating and scrubbing away
Layers of hurt
Damage and pain
Deleting and erasing
Learned behaviors
Trauma
Psychological and physical
Suffering
Wiping it down
To a clean canvas

My Sincere Thank You

Thank you God for all my blessings, past, present, and future. Continue to work in me and help me use my gifts to uplift your kingdom.

My family, thank you for not giving up on me, loving me unconditionally, giving me room to grow and make mistakes, attending my events and routing me on.

My church family, friends, and loved ones who continue to support me through this journey.

Counselors who put their patients first, and continue to encourage them to put in the work in order to heal.

All those creating spaces for poetry; allowing poets to practice and perfect their craft through features and open mics.

My fans who show tremendous love and support by attending my poetry performances and purchasing my books.

My son Mekhi, thank you for continuing to remind me that children are impacted, too, and adults need to say sorry when they are wrong. I love you for always speaking up.

My daughter Michelle Janayea and sister Madalena, you are truly appreciated. I would not be able to do what I do without you.

Journal Pages

Journal Pages

Journal Pages

Journal Pages

Journal Pages

Journal Pages

About the Author

Mariadaluz Fortes is a native of the Cape Verde Islands who migrated to the United States at the age of nine. During her teenage years she discovered her love for writing poetry. She concealed her naturally given talent and went on to find herself in adulthood. She received her Bachelors of Science in Business Administration at Providence College in Providence Rhode Island. In 2022 Mariadaluz used her writing as a way of healing herself and decided to share her gift with the world. Her goal is to continue writing about difficult topics, educating her readers and promoting counseling, open communication and healing. Further ensuring her community that seeking help is not a weakness. She is an active member of her church and a mother of two. She resides in Rhode Island.

Books by author:

Healing Through Poetry: Engagement Ring of Deception
Healing Through Poetry: Gift to My People
Healing Through Poetry: Beautiful Magical Scars

Made in the USA
Middletown, DE
02 May 2024